PRE-WAR 1619–1819

Seeds of War Sown Early!

I have been upr[…] Africa. After a horrible j[…] hold of a ship, here I am on t[…] land, at the hands of a white-s[…] I am their slave, that they can buy[…] Surely no good can come from such an idea.—**Ella**, August 1619, Jamestown, VA

We declare slavery illegal.

—Rhode Island, 1652

Slaves are hereby declared "real estate."

—State of Virginia, 1705

I is the Infant, from the arms
Of its fond mother torn,
And at a public auction sold
With horses, cows, and corn.

Z is a Zealous man, sincere,
Faithful, and just, and true;
An earnest pleader for the slave—
Will you not be so too?

I have frequently seen [slaves] whipt to that degree that large pieces of their skin have been hanging down their backs, yet I never observed one of them to shed a tear.—**John Brickell**

For months and months at a time we weren't allowed off the farm. Sometimes we would get as far as the gate and peep over. We were told that if we got outside the Padirollers would get us.—**Uriah Bennett**, slave

I haven't anything to say against slavery. My old folks put my clothes on me…they gave me shoes and stockings and put them on me when I was a little boy. I loved them, and I can't go against them in anything. There were things I did not like about slavery on some plantations, whuppin' and sellin' parents and children from each other, but I haven't much to say. I was treated good.

—Samuel Riddick

Slaves bring the judgment of Heaven on a country.—**George Mason**

I's just follow the finger. The white man point his finger and I follow it and do.—**Cuffee**, slave

In 1776 Thomas Jefferson signed the Declaration of Independence, which states "all men are created equal." Jefferson was a slave owner.

SOLD!

I didn't come to America to get along with other people from all over and from other states. What do I care about them? I came for opportunity for me and my family. I'm all for fast progress, and bigger cities, and more work. What do I have in common with those hick farmers in the South—nothing. To the Devil with them!—**blacksmith**, Rhode Island

I was an early victim of slave trading. I was born in Benin, in what is now Nigeria, in 1745. At age 11, I was kidnapped from my family and sold into slavery. Later I was sold again to traders and chained on a slave ship bound for America. I was sold to a Virginia planter, and then to a British naval officer, and finally to a Philadelphia merchant who gave me the chance to buy my freedom. As a ship's steward, I traveled widely. I also worked to bring an end to the slave trade. In 1791, I wrote my autobiography.—**Gustavus Vassa**

Laws, I gots to be up at dawn's crack with the baby to head to the fields. That sun sho is hot. Massa says we gots to pick fast today. Cotton is back-breakin' work. It's just one row after another. Gots to stop to nurse the baby as I can, but so the 'seer can't see me.—**Lizzie**, 17, plantation slave

Eli Whitney invents the cotton gin, 1793.

Eli Whitney's invention of the cotton gin made it possible for farmers to make more money and harvest more cotton each year. But it also meant farmers needed more workers. So, they bought slaves from Africa to tend their fields. The cotton gin revolutionized farming…and slavery.

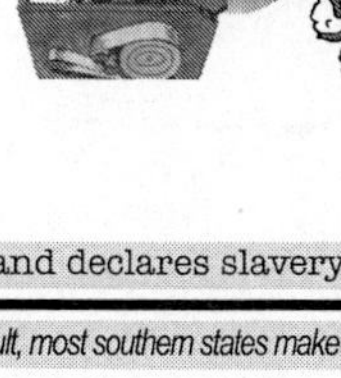

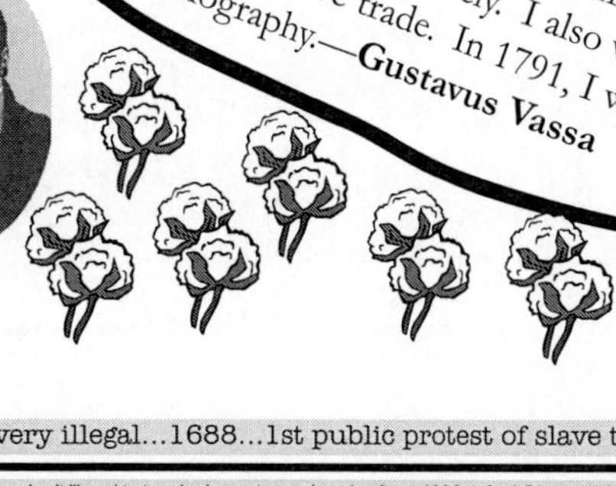

1619…1st slaves to America land in Virginia…1652…Rhode Island declares slavery illegal…1688…1st public protest of slave trade in Pennsylvania…1700

1829…A free black, David Walker, publishes an essay which encourages slaves to revolt. As a result, most southern states make it illegal to teach slaves to read and write…1830…Anti-Slavery Movement begins…1831…Maria Stewart is the first

The Fugitive Slave Act of 1793 demands the return of runaway slaves.

1820–1860 Antebellum="Before the War"

I don't know why some people can't understand the unity of the South. We have our own identity and traditions. Cotton is my crop and I need my slaves to make a successful living. If those darn Yankees came down here they'd see it's a lot of hot, hard hand-labor, no machine to magically get our crop in and meet the worldwide demand for cotton. Cotton is King, after all!—**plantation owner**, South Carolina

abolitionist: person who worked to do away with slavery

Slavery is a covenant with death and an agreement with hell.—abolitionist **William Lloyd Garrison**, *The Liberator,* Boston

COTTON IS KING!

Some people say "The South was built on the backs of blacks."

It's like this: they's good massas and bad massas. Most white folks not slaves, but be about as po' as we slaves are! My plantation family's good to me.—**slave cook**, Louisiana

Antislavery newspapers began in 1821 with white editor Benjamin Lundy's *Genius of Universal Emancipation*. It had six subscribers.

Reveille is a bugle call that was used to wake up sleeping soldiers at sunrise. During the Civil War, the call was sounded between 4:45-6:00 in the morning! When the last note played, the flag was raised, a gunshot was fired, and the soldiers had to be dressed and ready for roll call.

Slavery was sometimes called a "necessary evil" or the "peculiar institution."

A plot that involved 9,000 blacks, led by free black Denmark Vesey, was exposed in Charleston, South Carolina in 1822. Vesey and 36 others were executed.

I can't believe a man like that can be President of these United States! Andrew Jackson is nothing but a common man. Newspapers call him a "barbarian," "half-wit," and "tyrant," and I must say, I agree with them. The people got what they wanted, I guess…a low-class man running this whole nation!—**U.S. citizen**, 1828

Only one of every 20 Northerners was an active abolitionist.

I didn't have to be told that if a slave struck his master it meant death. Freeborn in North Carolina, but the son of a slave father, I knew slavery firsthand. My hatred of slavery drove me to Boston, where I sold old clothes and subscriptions to the *Freedom's Journal*. I burned to deliver my own message and in 1829 published my pamphlet, *Walker's Appeal*.—**David Walker**

In 1831, slave Nat Turner led 70 blacks in a revolt that slaughtered 57 men, women, and children in rural Southampton County, Virginia. Troops rushed in to put down the uprising and killed over one hundred blacks—the innocent as well as the insurrectionists—in a savage massacre. Wild rumors and alarms swept through the South—could this happen again?!—**newspaperman**, North Carolina

I didn't know I was a slave until I found out I couldn't do the things I wanted.—Edmund, Georgia

…Virginia declares slaves are "property"…New York puts runaway slaves to death…1725 …Virginia grants slaves right to form own church…1739…Slave

black woman to lecture against slavery…William Lloyd Garrison publishes the first edition of the newspaper, Liberator, which called for emancipation of slaves…Nat Turner leads a slave rebellion in Southampton, Virginia…1833…The American and

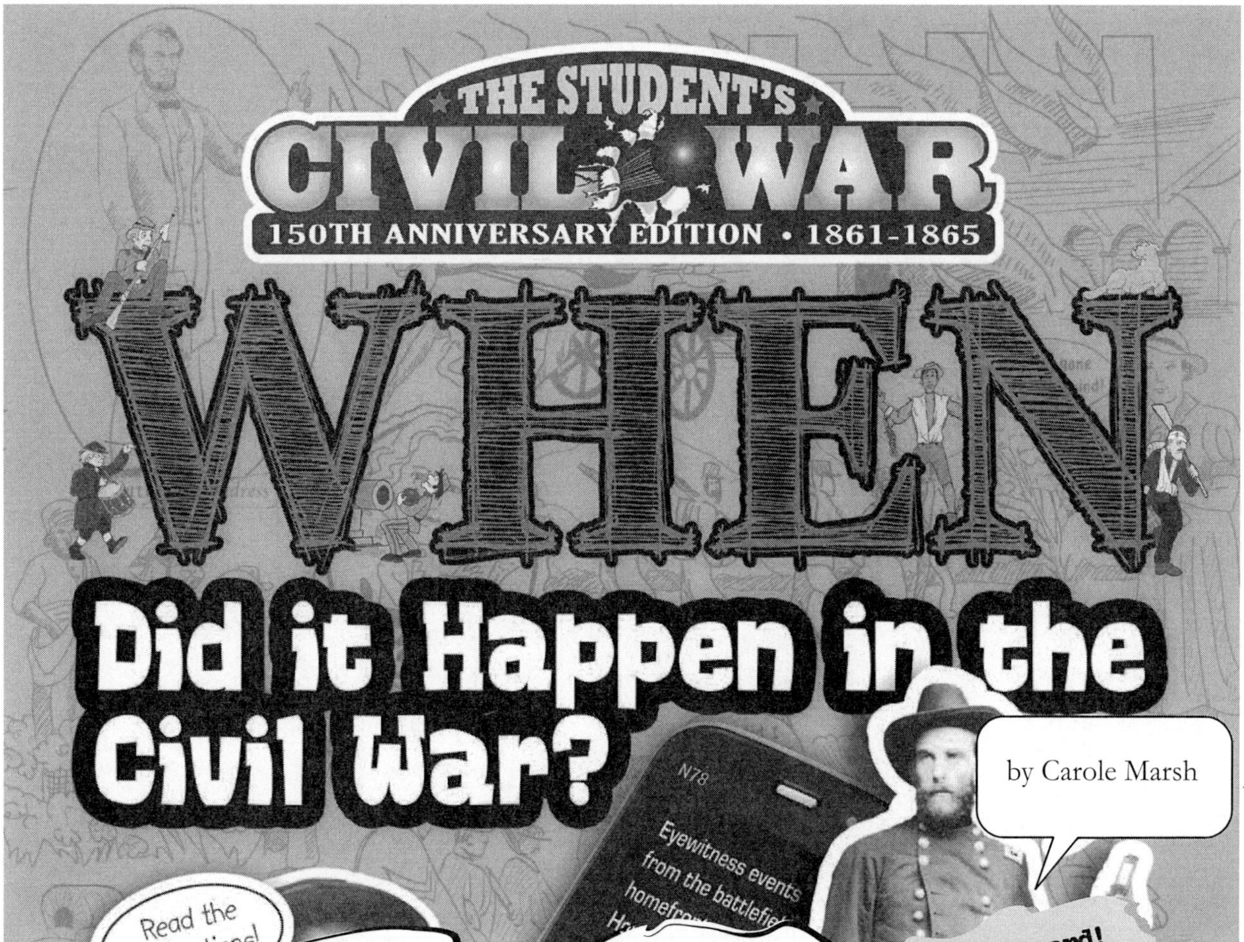

Southerners were polite in calling slavery a "necessary evil." I call slavery a "positive good." I stand by what I said in Congress—slavery is good for blacks!—**John C. Calhoun**, South Carolina senator, 1837

Boo!
Boo!

I was born a slave. I worked long and hard for my master 22 years. I finally ran away, and been hiding in a small space in my grandmother's attic for seven years. I'm trying to get to the North and gain my freedom. I finally have my chance. A boat is going to take me there tonight. Perhaps by morning, I'll be free!—**Harriet Jacobs**, North Carolina

How Come?

When I was born I was black.
When I grew up I was black.
When I'm sick I'm black.
When I go out into the sun I'm black.
When I die I'll be black.

But you:
When you were born you were pink.
When you grow up you are white.
When you get sick you are green.
When you go out in the sun you are red.
When you go out in the cold you are blue.
When you die you turn purple.
And you call me colored?

$50 Reward!

Ranaway from the Subscriber, living in the county of Edgecombe, NC, about eight miles north of Tarborough, on the 24th of August last, a negro fellow named Washington, about 24 years of age, 5 feet and 8 or 10 inches high, dark complexion, stout built, and an excellent field hand, no particular marks about him recollected.

Maybe he's on the railroad?

sesquicentennial: (noun) [ses-kwi-sen-ten-ee-uhl] a 150th anniversary or its celebration

Runaways Held in the New Bern, NC, Jail

Two New Negro Men, the one named Joe, about 45 years of age...much wrinkled in the face, and speaks bad English. The other is a young fellow...speaks better English than Joe, whom he says is his father, has a large scar on the fleshy part of his left arm.... They have nothing with them but an old Negro cloth jacket and an old blue sailor's jacket without sleeves. Also...a Negro named Jack, about 23 years of age...of a thin visage, blear-eyed...has six rings of his country marks around his neck, his ears are full of holes.

I was born on a plantation near Fayetteville, North Carolina, and I belonged to J.B. Smith. He owned about 30 slaves. When a slave was no good, he was put on the auction block in Fayetteville and sold.
—**Sarah Louise Augustus**

What man can make, man can unmake.—**Frederick Douglass**, abolitionist

rebellion in South Carolina; 44 slaves killed...1777...Vermont outlaws slavery...1783...Massachusetts outlaws slavery...1792...Kentucky joins Union as slave

the Female Anti-Slavery Societies are formed in Philadelphia...1833...Oberlin College is the first coed college founded to educate African Americans...1837...The first Anti-Slavery Convention of American Women is held in New

I thought it was the Year of the Tiger.
No, that was last year.
Oh.

It takes an army to do a book. Here's ours:

HEADQUARTERS
Gen. Michele Yother, Gen. Mike Longmeyer, Master Sergeant Cowboy Pilot Bob Longmeyer
Indispensible Right Hand (Wo)man: Nancy "You Gotta Have" Hart

All you really need is heart, you know.
I know.

CIVIL WAR CENTRAL
Chief Wrangler: Paige Muh
Sergeant at Art Arms: John Hanson
Scribes, First Class: Whitney Akin, Janice Baker, Sherri Smith Brown
(Battle) Field Artists: Vicki DeJoy, Corie Ferguson, Yvonne Ford, Randolyn Friedlander, Jessica Talley
Erstwhile Intern: Emily Kimbell

John's relative walked home from the Civil War.
Oh, I thought he drove a Volkswagon.

GENERAL & ACCOUNTING
Muster Masters: Marcie Comeau, Cindy Green, Bri Roden

That's the important people, right?
Absolutely.

SALES
Melessa Hill, Pam Morris, Gina Vranesevich, Lori White, Valerie Curry, Jennifer Johnson
Hallelujah Chorus: Denise Morris

War bonds, right?
Sure, wanna buy some?
Yeah, my old Confederate currency ok?

MARKETING MILITIA
Head of the One-Million-Man E-mail March: Camille Chasteen
Linda Metoyer, Mark Dean, Tammy Weeks, Jennifer Kelly, Justin Badger

PRODUCTION & FULFILLMENT
Colonel James Barnard
Dave Guerrero, Pernell Arnold, Kathy Morgan, Jeff Jerabeck

I need fulfilling.
You always do.

SPECIAL UNIT
Hair and Makeup: Christina Yother
Dance and Funny Faces: Grant Yother
Cheerleader: Avery Longmeyer
PT, Boot Camp, and Gymastics: Ella Longmeyer
Best Boy: Evan "Da? Da?!" Longmeyer

I could use a makeover.
Ya think?
My kinda guy!
Cute legs!
Whata sweetheart!
I thought he was the key grip.
That, too.

Private First Class: CAROLE MARSH

Shouldn't she go up at the top?
It's safer down here…out of the line of fire.
I'm just sayin…

In 1849, there were 15 Northern and 15 Southern states. There were more people in the North, but since each state had 2 senators, there was a "stalemate" in the Senate at that time for any effort to pass laws.

I remember all the bricklayers; they all was colored… The men that plastered the City Hall outside and put those columns up in the front…they was slaves, mos' all the fine work…was done by slaves. They called 'em artisans. None of 'em could read, but give 'em any plan an' they could foller it to the las' line.—**John H. Jackson**

Carole Marsh Civil War and Other Sassy Books for Young Readers are available from your favorite school supply or teacher store, almost all of America's fine museum and park stores, at lovely bookstores everywhere, or if all else fails, direct from www.gallopade.com, or call 1-800-536-2GET (that's 2438), extension 11, Miss Cindy.

For further information, trade terms, rights sales, good recipes, advice, and more, please contact:
GALLOPADE INTERNATIONAL
6000 Shakerag Hill
Suite 314
Peachtree City, Georgia
30269

You mean like when the wife stood on the hill and waved her hankie welcoming her Johnny home from the war?
The very same!
That's in the South, right?
Yes.
They made up that town name, right?
Probably.

See our bibliography and more at www.studentscivilwar.com

I had to try to put an end to this political battle! When the territory of California applied to join the Union in 1849—as a free state—the U.S. had half free and half slave states. To stop this madness, I introduced a bill that would let California be a free state. However, my Compromise of 1850 also said that any new state could choose to be free or slave based on "popular sovereignty" or what the people wanted. After all, a state should have the right to decide what it wants to be, right? My bill passed, but alas, it was only a temporary solution.—Senator **Henry Clay**, Kentucky

state…1793…The Fugitive Slave Act forces return of runaway slaves…Eli Whitney invents the cotton gin…1796…Tennessee joins Union as slave state…1800

York…1839…Joseph Cinque leads a successful revolt on the slave ship, Amistad…1850…Congress passes the Fugitive Slave Act requiring captured runaway slaves to be returned to their owners. Whites now hunt slaves for profit…

A Word from the Author

There's a song that goes *"War! What's it all about? Absolutely nothing!"*

However war is usually about *something*. As you know, the Revolutionary War was all about America wrenching herself away from the final grasp of her mother country of England. It was a war to secure freedom, a new nation, and a new way of life. Later, no one looked back and said, "Hey, maybe we shouldn't have fought that war."

Close to a hundred years after America's founding, people were restless. America was now about a lot of ways of life, many quite different from the others. You might be a plantation owner using slave labor to grow your cotton crop. You might be a mountain woman still living in the wilds of Appalachia. You could be a president trying to run the still new, young, ambitious, and sometimes, even cantankerous and disagreeable country.

Two of the major disagreements of the mid-1800s were slavery and states' rights versus federal rights. Some folks said that they could not survive without slave labor, that they were good to their slaves, and that slavery was now a necessary and permanent part of American life. Others said slavery was wrong and that there was no reason any human being should be owned by another. After all, wasn't America about freedom for all people?

Some Americans thought that states should be able to make their own decisions without so much interference from the federal government in Washington. (Sound familiar?) Other Americans insisted that's what Washington and the federal government were for: to keep all states fair and equal and to solve disputes.

You could say that lanky, teenage America had major growing pains! But America was no longer a "kid." America was at a serious crossroads. Would Americans fight their fellow Americans over these issues? Could such disagreements be resolved by talking, cooperation, compromise, and change? Or would we go to war?

What a curious turn of events—to believe you had to fight your fellow countrymen to the death! Wasn't there any other way? As we know today, getting along and solving problems is much better than going to war. Sometimes, if you are under attack, you may feel you have no choice but to go to war to defend your nation, or to defend others.

Let's just say it was complicated. By the spring of 1861, Americans were actually talking about going to war. They made it sound necessary, even exciting. Many believed it would be a quick war—with their side winning, naturally!

Of course, it didn't happen that way. It was a long war—four years—with terrible tragedies. Slavery was ended. But not before most people "took sides" and fought face-to-face, often against people they knew or were related to, until no one any longer felt that war was a good thing, not even a so-called "necessary" war.

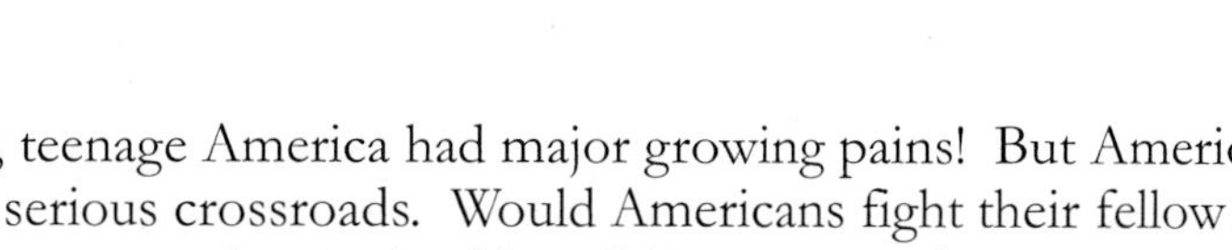

What eventually led to war was a long, drawn out, complex, contradictory set of circumstances, actions, misunderstandings, and oversights. Could we have ended slavery and preserved the union—without war? Think about this, for it may be your job to assess, decide, act or not act, or argue for or against some similar situation one day!

As you read, imagine being that person at that time, in that place during that event. How would you feel, what would you do, how would you change? Today, could we possibly still "stumble" into such a long war? Would around-the-clock news make a difference? Would gathering those who disagree around a table and negotiating work? Diplomacy? The Civil War contains a world of wondering!

What was the American Civil War about? What did it mean? Was there another way? Was it fun, exciting? Was it fair? Who won? Who lost? What would you have done? What do you think?

Why does it matter what *you* think? Because in the absence of diplomacy, cooperation, collaboration, compromise, understanding, honor, and integrity, it is war, not peace, that always looms on our horizon. The past was in their hands. The future is in yours.

Carole Marsh
Shakerag Hill
Peachtree City, Georgia

Reader,

After you read this book, you can go online to www.studentscivilwar.com and learn more.

Ask your school or public librarian to help you find resources for your age!

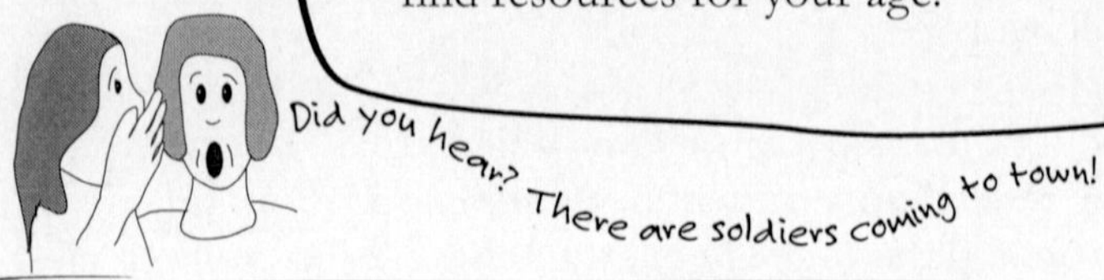

I've heard rumors of war going around lately. People whispering about soldiers, weapons, strategies. Some even say I've sparked their interest. They want to fight the South and end all the slavery right now. It's the book, I guess. When I wrote Uncle Tom's Cabin, I didn't expect it to be so controversial. I just knew the story needed to be told. I wanted people to know what life was really like for slaves, with good owners and bad owners from Southern and Northern towns. I think I really got people thinking. Most have never heard slavery described like this before.—**Harriet Beecher Stowe**

I am **Tom**, a fictional character from Ms. Stowe's famous book about how slaves were mistreated. In her story, I was murdered in cold blood by plantation overseer Simon Legree. Did such things happen in real life? Were they common or rare? What do you think?

I'm **Franklin Pierce**, elected president in 1852, but not strong enough to lead our nation through the gathering storm of war!

Nine months I was trying to get away.—**Solomon Northup**, slave, born free in New York, kidnapped in 1841 and enslaved on a cotton plantation near Red River in Louisiana.

I find it so hard to believe that Americans might fight Americans! North or South, we are all countrymen, neighbors, brothers, sisters, friends—how can war be? And yet I feel this volcanic groundswell growing beneath the very soil of the land. Will all these eternal arguments over slavery, state versus federal rights, and more just grow louder until we are not talking, but fighting?—**new mother**, Georgia

This footer is a Civil War timeline on top and an African American timeline on the bottom.

Territory, fueling debate over slave status...1808...Congress outlaws slave trade; slavery persists...1812...Louisiana joins Union as slave state...1816... Indiana

her first book of verse ...1857...With the Dred Scott Decision, the U.S. Supreme Court denies citizenship to black people...1859...White abolitionist, John Brown, leads a raid at Harper's Ferry. He is captured and sentenced to death...1861...Civil

The Civil War in a Nutshell...

In 1619 slaves were brought to America. *Hey, how come we have to be the slaves? Not sure, sorry.* Plantation owners in the South used slaves to grow crops like cotton. *Hey, Eli, hurry up and invent the cotton gin! Who's asking? Boll, Boll Weevil.* People in the North didn't grow many crops, they made things. *Like what?* Like shoes, clothes, railroads and things. *So they didn't need slaves?* No. Some thought slavery was wrong. They said so. *Abolitionists?* Yes. The South ignored them, said they'd always had slaves, and needed them. *Everyone in the South owned slaves?* No, very few did. *Everyone in the North opposed slavery?* No, but lots did. Americans also argued over whether the federal government...*That's Washington, DC, right?* Yes...or each state should have the most powerful laws. *Like about slavery?* Like about slavery. New states joined as Free states or Slave states. Senator Henry Clay made a compromise law so states could decide for themselves. Some people didn't like this and kept fighting over whether slavery was right or wrong. John Brown tried to lead a slave revolt. It didn't work. He was hanged for breaking the law. But people couldn't forget him. In 1860 Abraham Lincoln was elected president. Abe was against slavery and everybody knew it. That made some people happy and others UNhappy. That same year, South Carolina said, "We don't wanna be part of the United States of America anymore!" Other states also seceded. *How could they do that?* They just did, even though it was illegal. Abe had a problem. The country was dividing into pieces. Georgia, Louisiana, Florida, South Carolina, Alabama, Mississippi, Virginia, Texas, Arkansas, North Carolina, and Tennessee became the Confederate States of America under the leadership of Jefferson Davis. They made their own flag. *The Rebel flag, right?* Right, and their own government. That very year, Confederates-some called 'em Rebels-and the Union-some called 'em Yanks-met up at Fort Sumter in South Carolina. With one shot **BOOM!** the Civil War officially began! No one was killed but it excited lots of people. Soldiers came from everywhere! Boys, men, teenagers, grandpas, fathers, sons, brothers, uncles, even some girls *wanted* to fight. Soldiers picked their side-North or South-and joined the army. The first battle was at Bull Run, or Manassas, depending on whether you're a Yankee or Southerner. Confederates won, hands down. Next came battle after battle. There was a battle between two iron ships, the *Monitor* and the *Merrimac*. Then Battle of Shiloh, Seven Days Battle, Second Battle of Bull Run, and Battle of Antietam, bloodiest of the Civil War. There were soldiers fighting battles all over. While one was happening on a field in Virginia, another was happening by a creek in Alabama. There were too many to count! In 1863, Lincoln issued the Emancipation Proclamation. It said all slaves were free. The slaves *loved* it, the North *loved* it, the South *hated* it! Fighting continued in Chancellorsville, Tennessee. General Stonewall Jackson was hit **POW**! He died a few days later. Soldiers fought a bloody battle at Gettysburg, Pennsylvania. Thousands died on both sides. But the Union said they won. The Union had been losing most battles and wanted to quit. But Gettysburg revived their spirits. They fought in Vicksburg, Mississippi, such a long battle people ate rats! *Ewww!* And Chickamauga. On November 19, 1863, President Lincoln gave the Gettysburg Address and said "all men are created equal." *Even slaves?* Especially slaves. The South still didn't agree. The Civil War kept going. General Ulysses S. Grant became head of the Union army. He led troops through the Battle of the Wilderness and finally to Petersburg Virginia. The Union backed the Confederates into a corner. It was...quiet...no...gunshots...cannons... or fighting. Soldiers stared at each other...waiting...waiting...waiting for someone to make a move. While those soldiers waited in Virginia, other Confederates tried to protect Atlanta, Georgia from the Yankees. General William T. Sherman led Union soldiers toward Atlanta. The Rebels ***PUSHHHEEEDDD*** against Sherman. Sherman ***PUSHHHEEEDDD*** against the Rebels. Sherman won. He burned Atlanta to the ground! Then he *walked* through almost the whole state with his entire army. He ended up in Savannah, Georgia, which he "gave" to President Lincoln as a Christmas gift! Back in Petersburg, those soldiers were *still* staring at each other until the Confederates tried to protect an important railroad station. They failed. They marched to Richmond, Virginia with the Union on their heels. Richmond was the Confederate States of America's capital. The soldiers, led by General Robert E. Lee, did all they could to protect Richmond. They failed. They kept marching backwards, slowly running from the Union. The Confederates ended up at Appomattox Court House, Virginia. Robert E. Lee had nowhere to turn. He didn't want more men to die. He surrendered. Lee and Grant met. Lee signed surrender papers. Grant said Lee was dignified and took defeat gracefully. *So the war was over?* Yes, officially, but some battles continued until the word got around. By the time the four year war was over, more than 618,000 men had died. It took years to rebuild the South and help the slaves learn how to be free. But the United States was one nation again. *What did the soldiers do?* They went home.

joins Union as free state...1817...Mississippi joins Union as slave state...1818...Illinois joins Union as free state...1819...Alabama joins Union as slave state...

War begins...Charlotte Forten Grimke becomes a volunteer teacher of freed men on St. Helena Island in South Carolina...1863...Harriet Tubman leads a military raid on the Combahee River in South Carolina and helps hundreds of slaves escape

THE CIVIL WAR was four long years of bloodshed, battles, victories, and devastating defeats. A brand new America, less than 100 years old, wasn't getting along. They had disagreements about states' rights and slavery. But, instead of sitting around the dinner table and talking their problems out, our young country decided to settle their disagreements with a fight. Little did they know the fight would last years and kill thousands of fathers, sons, brothers, and friends.

The Civil War was a HUGE part or our nation's history, but sometimes, it's just downright hard to understand! We know it was long. We know it was violent. We know the North and South fought. But do we really know WHAT happened WHEN?

Well it's about time we figured that out! So, strap on your best imaginary helmet and get ready to take a ride down the timeline of the Civil War. There'll be stops along the way, so remember to listen (and read!)

The term Civil War means a war between citizens (or CIVILians) in the same country.

The North generally refers to states north of the Ohio River, and the South generally refers to states south of the Ohio River.

1820...The Missouri Compromise admits Maine to Union as free state, Missouri as slave state, and prohibits slavery north of Missouri...1821... Missouri

to freedom...1865...The Thirteenth Amendment abolishes slavery...The Freedmen's Bureau is established by Congress...1872...The Freedmen's Bureau is abolished by Congress...1877...The Hayes Compromise ends Reconstruction by

We're not part of your Union anymore.
GA
We'll make our own country!
MS
We have the right, we're states!
LA
I will have slaves if I darn well please!
VA
You brought war on yourself when you elected that Lincoln!
AR
God is on our side!
TN
No one in Washington will tell me how to run my life!
SC
1861 after the election of Abraham Lincoln as president, Southern states began to secede from the Union.
You Yankees don't know nothin'!
FL
Our tea may be sweet but our fightin' is sour!
AL
You best know, Southern loyalty's strong!
NC
We fight with Southern pride!
TX
The first state to secede from the Union was South Carolina.
A total of 11 states seceded from the Union.
I don't agree with slavery ... but the South is my home and I've got to fight for Virginia!
Virginia's part of the Union. We shouldn't have left. I'm fighting for the Union!
Southern states did not think their economy and businesses could survive without slaves.
Seccession from the United States of America was considered illegal.
SOUTHBOY: I'm confused
NORTHGUY: y?
SOUTHBOY: r we fighting each other?
NORTHGUY: u r confederate, i am union
SOUTHBOY: but u r my BFF!
NORTHGUY: sry! I luv the north
SOUTHBOY: hope we don't fight each other!
NORTHGUY: me 2
SOUTHBOY: I won't shoot at u if u won't shoot at me!
NORTHGUY: deal
SOUTHBOY: k, ttyl
NORTHGUY: bye!

1861 February

the Southern states elected **Jefferson Davis** to be **president** of their newly formed country, the **Confederate States of America.**

Warbook | Search | Home | Profile | Account

NEWS FEED

Jefferson Davis is excited to be president of the Confederate States of America!

12,000 people like this

View all 100 comments

Jo Bob we're rooting for you Jeff!

Ellie Clements us women are on your side, President Davis!

Bubba yeeehaaaw for the South!!!!

Write a comment ...

The Confederate capital was first in Montgomery, Alabama, then moved to Richmond.

Requests

Franklin Pierce
add as friend

Southern militia began taking over Union military posts in the South.

front porch rocking chairs

Confederate Capital*

*Capital tours only $9.99 per person

Visit beautiful Richmond, Virginia

home of southern belles

FIRST SHOTS FIRED AT FORT SUMTER!

WANTED

All southern gentlemen, farmers, slaves, and businessmen able to fight.
Young and old.
Bring own weapon.
Thousands needed.

The battle at Fort Sumter lasted 36 hours until the Union lowered its flag in defeat.

1861

April 12, 1861, the first shot of the Civil War was fired at Fort Sumter, South Carolina.

The attack on Fort Sumter was considered an act of war by President Abraham Lincoln.

No one was killed in battle at Fort Sumter.

The first shot was fired by Confederates.

TELEGRAM

The Western Union Telegraph Company
Received at
Fort Sumter, South Carolina
April 12, 1861

SOS stop Shots at Ft. Sumter stop
Union needs backup stop The war has
begun stop
Fort Commander

Dearest Jane,

Sweat clouds my eyes as I write to you. The summer heat is bearing down hard. Tomorrow, Gen. McDowell will lead us Union Troops toward Manassas. The battle will be even and I am confident the North will win. I carry your love with me always. I can only hope to see you soon.

All my love,
Jonathon

Battle of Manassas is a success for the Confederacy. Small time commander Thomas Jackson received credit as best officer in battle. Coined with nickname "Stonewall" from army. "Stonewall" Jackson declared a hero!

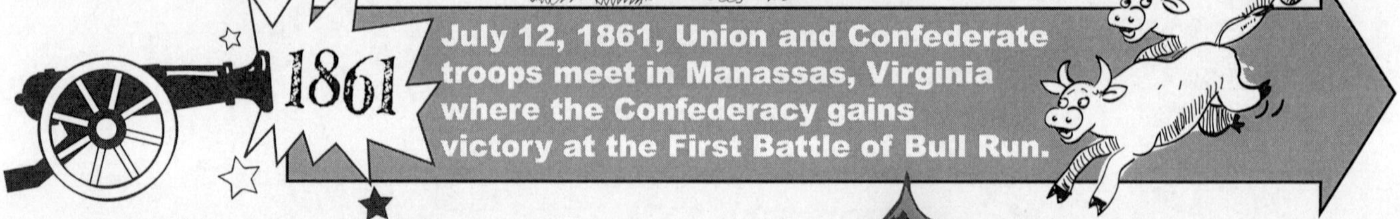

Sent: July 21, 1861, 5:15 p.m.

To: samsoldier@confederacy.com

From: maybelle@confederacy.com

Subject: Battle of Bull Run

Sam! The battle of Bull Run was nothing like I expected it to be. I came to sit on the hill and watch it. I thought it would be entertaining...it wasn't. It was horrifying! I saw so many people die. I couldn't see you from way up there, but I know you are in Gen. Jackson's division. Email me back as soon as you get this and let me know if you're OK.

I miss you big brother!

Maybelle

Northern industry...South Carolina nullifies federal edict, calls for secession...President Jackson declares no states may leave Union...1833...Lucretia Mott

Southern states to gather life histories of ex-slaves...1940...Ella Jo Baker, a dedicated organizer in the freedom movement, begins work in the South as field secretary of the NAACP...1941...Civil Rights Movement begins...Thousands of black

the battle between the Union's Monitor and the Confederate's Merrimac is the first between

ironclad ships.

March, 1862

UNION

THE MONSTER SHIP IS OUT!

pp. 55-58

- how will the Union fight back?
- does the Union have an ironclad ship?
- how much damage can the Confederacy do?

The *Merrimac* was also called the *Virginia*.
The battle was a draw.

forms Female Anti-Slavery Society…Theodore Weld forms American Anti-Slavery Society…Ohio's Oberlin College 1st to admit blacks…1835… South Carolina

people organize to press their demands for justice… President Roosevelt issues an executive order against discrimination of workers in defense industries and government…1942… Margaret Walker wins the Yale Award for Young Poets for her

1862
April 6-7

Confederate and Union troops fight along the Tennessee River in the Battle of Shiloh

The Battle of Shiloh was the first time many soldiers realized how long and bloody the Civil War would be.

Susan,

I am sorry. I could not stomach the blood and death. I shamefully deserted the Union Army at the Battle of Shiloh. I cannot return home. Everyone will call me a traitor. I will hide until the war is over and find you then. Please keep this a secret.

Yours truly,
Charles

26 JUNE | 27 JUNE | 28 JUNE | 29 JUNE | 30 JUNE | 1 JULY | 2 JULY

1862 June 26, 1862, the Seven Days Battles begin near the Confederate capital, Richmond, Virginia

Orders from Jefferson Davis. Gen. Robert E. Lee will replace Gen. Johnston.

generalspace

Home | Browse People | Find Friends | Local | Music

RICHMOND, VA
United States

Profile Views: 100,015

Last Login: 4/20/1862

Robert E. Lee: General Info
Member Since: 1/19/1807
Website: N/A
Influences: Father, major-general Henry Lee
Education; West Point Military School, Class 1829
Hometown: Westmoreland County, Virginia
Wife: Mary Custis Lee
Career: Commanding General, Confederate Army

MAC'S ARTILLERY SUPPLY

more BANG for your buck
Manager - Billy Bob White
Richmond, Virginia

10,000 muskets	$150.00
50 barrels gun powder	$100.00
50 cannons	$200.00
5 boxes cannon balls	$54.99

20,000 Confederate soldiers died and 16,500 Union soldiers died.

...Arkansas joins Union as slave state...1837...Michigan joins Union as free state...1845...Florida joins Union as slave state...Texas joins union as slave state

Truman issues an executive order banning segregation in the armed forces...Pharmacist Ella Nora Phillips Stewart is elected president of the National Association of Colored Women...Edith Irby Jones is the first black to be admitted to a Southern

hitter

Home Profile Find People Settings Help

What's happening?

```
Discover what battles are happening right now,
anywhere in the war
```

Home

Tweet!

Tweet!

TotallyUnion The Union Army is just outside Richmond with Gen. McClellan.

clearlYconfederatE Gen. Johnston was hurt in battle a month ago ☹ Gen. Lee is our new commander, we've been gatherin' supplies for a fight!

RevelDaze We've got 85,000 men, them Yanks got 115,000. But that don't matter, we're gonna win. We're goin' after them Yanks at Mechanicsville, just outside of Richmond, VA!

YankTank The Confederates are winning, then the Union, then the Confederates...This battle is lasting forever...guess that's why they're calling it The Seven Days Battles!

SonoftheSouth we pushed them darn Yanks back, took over their supply, and left 'em runnin' toward Washington, D C with their tails between their legs! YEEEHAAW!

Peace<3er I saw the 7 days battle from the sidelines. The Confederates may have won, but both sides lost. 16,000 in Union dead. 20,000 Confederates dead.

1862 August 1862, Confederates attack Union troops at Manassas, VA in the Second Battle of Bull Run.

The Second Battle of Bull Run/Manassas was fought in the same place as the First Battle of Bull Run.

Confederates won for the second time at Bull Run/Manassas.

At the next hill, turn left.
Walk 7.6 miles, then turn right.
Arrive at destination on left.
You have arrived at the battlefield of Manassas/Bull Run.

TELEGRAM

The Union Telegraph Company
Received at
Battlefield of Manassas, Virginia
August, 1862

President Lincoln stop Official field report stop Confederate victory stop 14,000 Union dead stop 9,000 Confederate dead stop failure for Union stop

Gen. McClellan

FROM THE DESK OF GENERAL MCCLELLAN...

Remember, the Army of the Potomac is the best army in the Union ... thanks to me!

Don't forget! Second Battle of Manassas, travel to Virginia tomorrow.

Note to self: Cannot let any men in Army of Potomac die. Must keep the army safe at all costs.

Gen. Stonewall Jackson's surprise attacks on Union troops sparked the battle.

Men, it's up to us to defeat Gen. Pope's Union Army before Gen. McClellan's men arrive. They're coming on boat right up to Richmond.

So here's the plan, men. We'll defeat Pope's army while they're alone. Then we'll be waiting for McClellan and his men when he gets here. We'll send a surprise shiver right up his spine!

1850...Congress passes the Compromise of 1850...1852...Harriet Beecher Stowe publishes Uncle Tom's Cabin...1854...Congress passes the Kansas-Nebraska

deliberate speed."...In Montgomery, Alabama, Rosa Parks refuses to give up her seat on a public bus to a white man. She is arrested and jailed...A year-long bus boycott results in the U.S. Supreme Court invalidating segregation on Montgomery

1862 September

Confederate troops head into Union territory to fight the

Battle of Antietam in Maryland

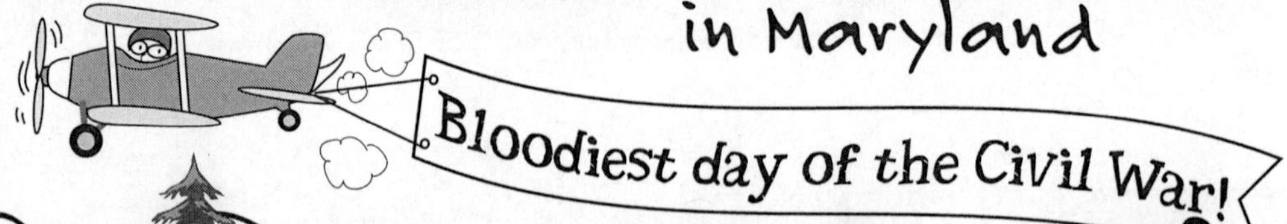

Official Confederate battle plans from Robert E. Lee: Head north through Maryland toward the Potomac River. Capture Harper's Ferry.

MCCLELLAN'S TELLIN'S blog

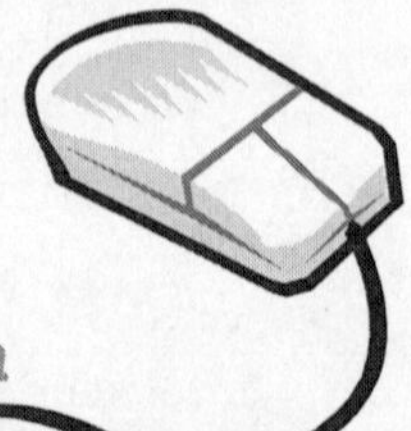

September, 1862

Battle of Antietam

Some may think I'm a coward, but I can't risk defeat. I won't destroy the Army of the Potomac just for pride and power. I have reason to believe that Gen. Lee's troops greatly outnumber our own. I will not fight against a bigger enemy. It is certain defeat.

view older blog posts ...

Act…1856…Proslavery candidate James Buchanan elected president…1857…Supreme Court rules escaped slave Dred Scott is property that must be returned

buses...1957…As president of the state NAACP, Daisy Gatson Bates leads the fight for school integration in Little Rock, Arkansas…1960…First student sit-ins at a lunch counter in Greensboro, North Carolina…1961…More than 50,000 people

1862

September 22, 1862, President Lincoln issues the Emancipation Proclamation as an official order to end the war.

According to the Union, all Southern slaves were considered free in 1863.

President Lincoln has ordered that all Southern States rejoin the Union by January 1, 1863. On that date, all slaves in the South will be free by the order of this great Union.

Free slaves began joining the Union Army to fight against the South.

Warbook

Search

NEWS FEED

South Master can't believe that Lincoln thinks he can boss me around. He's got another thing commin'! I ain't givin' up my slaves.

9,985 people like this

View all 100 comments

Southern Slave is excited about Lincoln's Emancipation Proclamation! I can't wait to be free! Check out the link to read more! www.emancipationproclamation.com

Southern slave **became a fan of** Association of Free Southern Slaves

Southern slave **and** Abraham Lincoln **are now friends.**

Southern Master **joined the group** 10,000 Warbook fans against Lincoln!

Write a comment ...

1862

Oct-Dec

Battle of Perryville

Union and Confederate troops continue fighting battles across the South from Kentucky to Tennessee.

The Battle of Murfreesboro was fought on the last day of 1862, December 31.

December

Battle of Murfreesboro

hitter

Home Profile Find People Settings Help

What's happening?

Discover what battles are happening right now, anywhere in the war

Tweet!

Home

Tweet!

OhioMama can't believe how many Union soldiers died down in Murfreesboro!

GAboy WOOHOO! Victory is sweeeeeet!

FrankTheYank wants this war to end. Why can't Lincoln choose some decent generals??

election to Senate...1859...Oregon joins Union as free state...Abolitionist John Brown leads slave revolt; Brown is hanged...1860...Antislavery candidate

the first black woman to receive a degree from the University of Georgia...1964... Fannie Lou Hamer is a founder and vice chairperson of the Mississippi Freedom Democratic Party...1964...The Civil Rights Act prohibits discrimination in public

1863 May

Confederates gain victory at the Battle of Chancellorsville but lose their great General Stonewall Jackson.

10 day weather report

Tonight	rain, rain, rain
Sun	rain, rain, rain
Mon	rain, rain, rain
Tue	rain, rain, rain
Wed	rain, rain, rain
Thu	rain, rain, rain
Fri	rain, rain, rain
Sat	rain, rain, rain
Sun	rain, rain, rain
Mon	rain, rain, rain

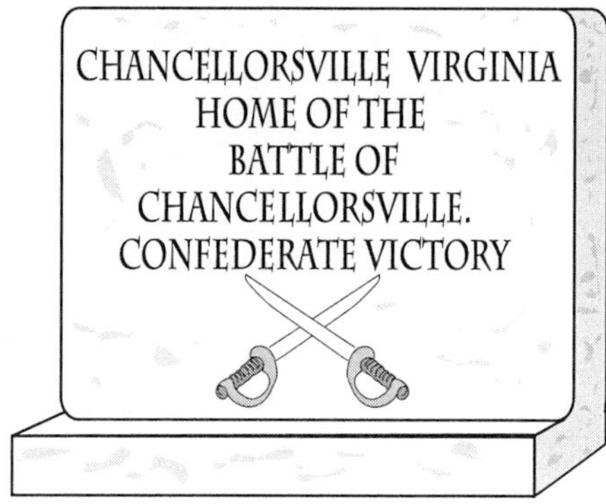

Beware of surprise attacks.

Battle of Gettysburg

1863

July 3, 1863, Union victory at the Battle of Gettysburg, Pennsylvania marks a turning point in the Civil War.

TRAIN 241

DEPARTING:
GETTYSBURG, PENNSYLVANIA
DESTINATION: VIRGINIA

Status: Full, 22,000 Confederate bodies on board to be returned home to bury

THE JOURNEY OF A CONFEDERATE GENERAL

blog

July, 1863

My Strategies

I feel the best way to continue to have the upper hand in this war is to wage battle on Northern ground. So far, we have only had victory in the South. If we can win a battle in the North we can lower Northern morale and raise Southern confidence.

view older blog posts ...

Sent: July 30, 1863, 5:15 p.m.
To: bobsoldier@confederacy.com
From: johnsoldier@confederacy.com
Subject: Yanks at Gettysburg!

Bob,

Me an' a group of other guys went up to Gettysburg to try an' find some shoes. Our feet's been real sore, brother! While we were there, we saw a whole bunch of Union troops. They're gathered at Gettysburg. We pulled back an' hid in the woods!

John

Sent: July 30, 1863, 5:17 p.m.
To: johnsoldier@confederacy.com
From: bobsoldier@confederacy.com
Subject: REPLY: Yanks at Gettysburg!

John,

Stay put. I told Gen. Lee an' we're comin' up that way. Looks like we're in for another battle!

Bob

GETTYSBURG IN HISTORY

it was a Union victory in reality, it was a battle that no one won

Over 23,000 Union soldiers were killed or wounded at the Battle of Gettysburg.

1863 July Battle at Vicksburg

Gen. Grant's Union troops surround Vicksburg, Mississippi, cut off all supplies to the town, and wait for Confederates to surrender.

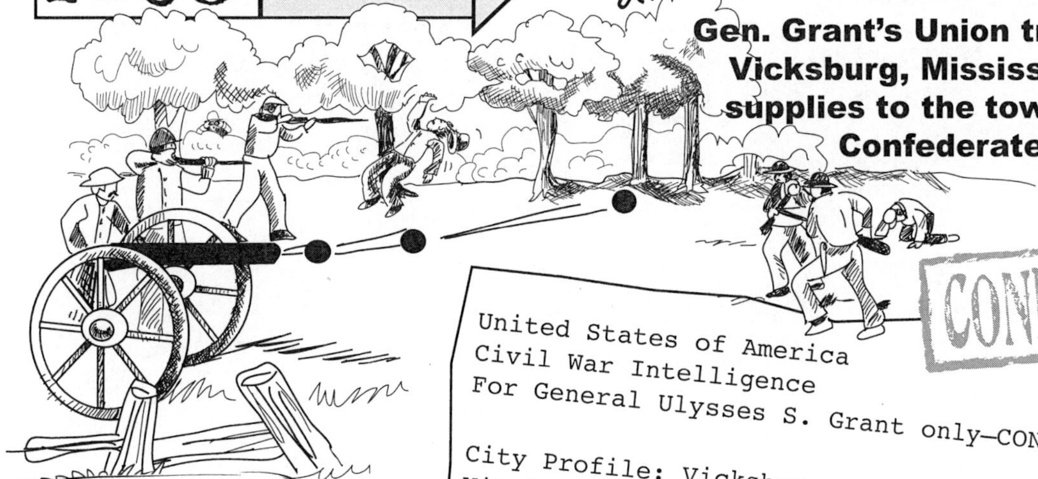

CONFIDENTIAL

United States of America
Civil War Intelligence
For General Ulysses S. Grant only—CONFIDENTIAL

City Profile: Vicksburg, Mississippi
Vital to Western Theatre. Must take city in order to split the Confederacy. Must destroy supply lines. DANGER: city located on Mississippi River. Use extreme caution when crossing the river. Plan strategically to overtake Confederate troops.

With no food supply, people in Vicksburg began to eat mules, dogs, and even rats!

Dear Diary,
We've been trying to hold Vicksburg for a month. We have no food, we're dirty, some people are eating rats just to survive! I'd rather someone just win already so we can go home in peace.

People inside Vicksburg hid in basements, hills, and caves to get away from Union attacks.

Should I take the risk and cross the Mississippi River to capture Vicksburg?

Pros
- control of Western Confederacy
- cut off Confederate supply line
- victory for Union

Cons
- difficult to cross
- men will be killed
- could be failure for Union

1863 Battle of Chickamauga

Sept. 19-20

Confederate troops block the Union's advance toward Atlanta at Chickamauga, Georgia.

The Battle of Chickamauga was the most significant Union defeat in the Civil War.

September 19, 1863

Official Union Battle Strategy

We suspect the Confederate Army has been split. Head south through the mountains of Georgia. Go in small groups to travel through narrow valleys and hills. Attack when fired upon. Expect easy win.

General Rosecrans

Battle plans

Many Union soldiers abandoned the army and ran in retreat toward Chattanooga, Tennessee.

September 19, 1863

Official Confederate Battle Strategy

The Union will follow us south through Georgia. Be prepared. Gather army into strong force. Do not split apart. We will be waiting for Union troops.

General Bragg

Chickamauga is a name given to a river by Indians that means "River of Death."

General Bragg led Confederate troops and General Rosecrans led Union troops.

Chickamauga—chick uh maw guh—1: a small town in north Georgia. 2: Civil War battle where Confederates gained victory under Gen. Bragg. Defeated Gen. Rosecrans and Union.

officially begins…Federal Navy blockades Southern ports…Virginia, Arkansas, North Carolina, and Tennessee join Confederacy…Union defeated at Battle of

York elects Shirley Chisholm as first African American U.S. Congresswoman…1969…Mary Moultrie leads a wage strike at the Medical College Hospital in South Carolina...1972… Political activist and intellectual, Angela Davis is acquitted of murder

Gettysburg Address

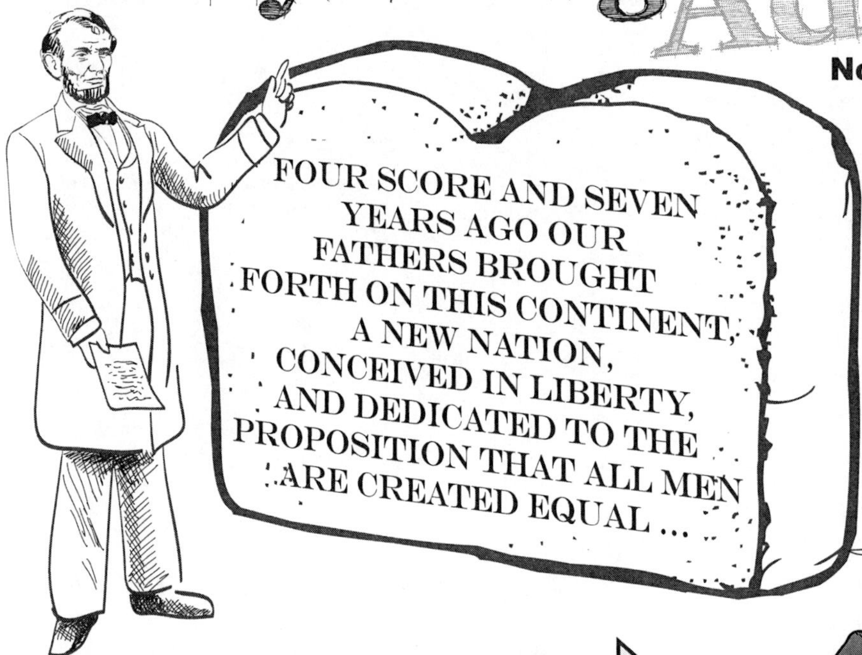

November 1863, President Lincoln gives the Gettysburg Address to honor the thousands of fallen soldiers.

1863 November

Confederate soldiers surround Chattanooga, Tennessee in an unsuccessful siege.

DAILY NEWS

UNDER SIEGE!

Chattanooga will enter its second month under siege. With Confederate control of Chattanooga, Union civilians and soldiers are starved and weary.

WARNING!

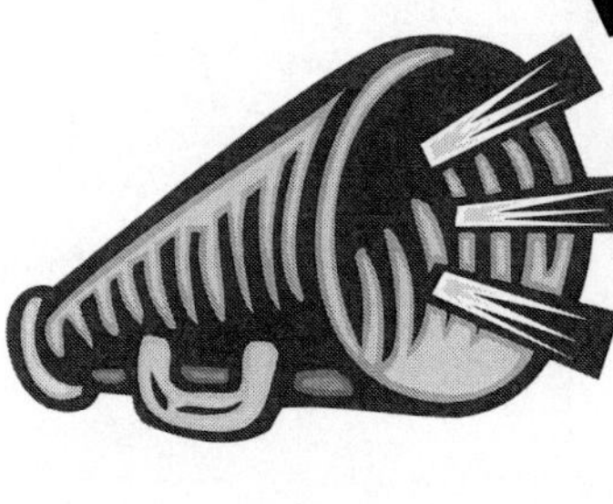

GRANT, HOOKER, AND SHERMAN are on their way to Chattanooga to defend the Union!

1863 1864 General Grant is appointed commander of the Union Army

generalspace

People

Home | Browse People | Find Friends | Local | Music | Games | Events

WASHINGTON, D.C.
United States

Profile Views: 215,487

Last Login: 1/10/1864

Ulysses S. Grant: General Info
Member Since: 4/27/1822
Website: N/A
Influences: Gen. Zachary Taylor
Education: West Point Military School, Class 1843
Hometown: Georgetown, Ohio
Wife: Julia Boggs Dent
Career: Commanding General, Union Army

1864 Union and Confederate troops fight in the thick woods of Virginia in the ...

Battle of the Wilderness

Sent: May 6,1864, 12:00 a.m.
To: marycustis@confederacy.com
From: genroblee@confederacy.com
Subject: bitter sweet victory

Mary,

I should be celebrating as my men are tonight. The Confederates won at the Battle of the Wilderness. Still, I cannot bring myself to even smile while thousands of young men lay dead on the battlefield. This war is so cruel. Stay safe and keep the light on for me, I hope to be home soon.

Robert

1864 Aug-Sept

Union and Confederate troops surround Petersburg, Virginia in a Siege of Petersburg

Gen. Grant planned to keep Petersburg under siege until the town was low in supplies and strength.

HA! YOU BLINKED!

In a siege, each side waits for the other to make the first move.

The Yankees have arrived in Petersburg, Virginia

Petersburg, Virginia was a very important city because it was home to a Southern railroad hub.

Where the Confederate railroads* meet.
Where supplies are shipped south.
Where Confederates do business.
Only miles from the capital, Richmond, VA

*railroad tours $15.00 per person.
Union Army not permitted.
Children under 12 free

Petersburg, Virginia

meanwhile...

Atlanta Campaign

1864 May

Gen. Sherman's Union troops fight their way through Georgia and take over Atlanta.

ATLANTA DAILY

EVACUATE!

Escape Plan
-why some are heading south, west, east, even north!

City Under Fire
-what to do when they come for you

WANTED

the city of
Atlanta, Georgia
dead or alive
reward:
Union Victory

Citizens were forced to evacuate Atlanta.

**This just in!
Yankees in Atlanta!
Cannon shots heard
on the outskirts of town!**

REBELJO: Our main goal in GA is 2 stop Sherman from coming South
CONFEDTED: y?
REBELJO: if he comes S he will get ATL
CONFEDTED: what happens when he gets ATL?
REBELJO: Sherman will ttly destroy it!
CONFEDTED: y?
REBELJO: b/c ATL is important 2 Confed.
CONFEDTED: omg, we have 2 protect ATL!
REBELJO: right! g2g. ttyl!
CONFEDTED: k, cu l8r

1864 November

The Union reelects Abraham Lincoln as President of the United States

U.S. Capitol
East Capitol Street, NE and 1st Street, NE
Washington, D.C. 20002

Reelection Inaugural Speech Enclosed
Attn: President Abraham Lincoln
1600 Pennsylvania Ave NW
Washington D.C. 20006

Citizens in the South did not consider Lincoln to be their president.

Lincoln was the first president to be assassinated while in office.

hitter

Home Profile Find People Settings Help

What's happening?

Discover what battles are happening right now, anywhere in the war

Tweet!

Top hits

Tweet!

StinkinLincoln I really can't stand that man, who would elect him again?

NoFightingAllowed Lincoln has only brought war to this country. He won't get my vote!

FrEeSlavEgUrL Lincoln gave me freedom, now I have a life of my own. I'll vote for him!

unionman just give him a chance! Lincoln will win this war. No doubt in my mind.

Gettysburg Address...Union forces gain control Tennessee...1864...Grant appointed commander of Union Army...General Sherman conquers Atlanta, Georgia

tournaments...Talk show host Oprah Winfery receives the first Bob Hope Humanitarian Award at the 54th Annual Emmy Awards...Halle Berry becomes first African American to win an Academy Award for best actress...The Slavery Reparations

...Maryland abolishes slavery...Nevada joins union as free state...Abraham Lincoln wins reelection as president...Sherman begins "March to the Sea" through

Coordinating Committee, led by prominent African American lawyers and activists, announce plans to sue companies that profited from slavery... President George W. Bush awards comedian and actor Bill Cosby and baseball player Hank Aaron

Sherman's March to the Sea ends in Savannah, Georgia

It took years to rebuild the damage Gen. Sherman did to Georgia. :(

TELEGRAM

The Union Telegraph Company
Received at
Savannah Telegraph Office
December, 21, 1864

Savannah is ours! stop Merry Christmas stop

General Sherman

After the March to the Sea, many women and children were left with no food and clothing for the winter.

Dearest Tom,

I hope your battlefield finds you in better condition than here in Albany, GA. Our house has been robbed and destroyed by Union troops. There is nothing left of the home we once had. Now Sarah and I, she only 3 months old, must survive the winter with no food, blankets, or supplies. Please, Tom, come home soon! NOW!

Elizabeth

Gen. Sherman offered the town of Savannah to President Lincoln as a Christmas gift.

Gen. Sherman did not destroy Savannah because of its beauty.

Georgia…1865…Robert E. Lee appointed general-in-chief of all Confederate armies…Missouri abolishes slavery…Abraham Lincoln rejects Jefferson Davis's

the nation's highest civilian honor—the Presidential Medal of Freedom…2005…Condoleezza Rice is appointed Secretary of State becoming the first African American woman to serve as Secretary of State…Hurricane Katrina hits southern coast

And We're Back!

1865 January

Siege at Petersburg continues

Sent: January, 10 1865, 6:30 a.m.

To: allsoldiers@confederacy.com

From: genroblee@confederacy.com

Subject: Time to move!

Soldiers,

We have waited here in Petersburg long enough. We must make a move or we will die old men in these trenches. On my order, we will fight back to protect Richmond and defeat those Yankees!

Gen. Lee

From the desk of
President Jefferson Davis

To Whom It May Concern:
I regret to inform the Confederacy that the city of Richmond, our Confederate Capital, has been overtaken by Union soldiers. The government and I will move to a safe location until Richmond is ready to occupy once again. Do not be discouraged, the Confederacy is still strong!

Jefferson Davis

peace proposals…13th Amendment to Constitution abolishes slavery…Confederates forced into full retreat…Confederate general Robert E. Lee surrenders to

of the United States…Ceremonial groundbreaking of the African Burial Ground in Manhattan takes place—the site will serve as memorial to 17th-18th century African slaves…Forbes magazine ranks Condoleezza Rice as the most powerful

1865 April

Confederate troops retreat to Appomattox Court House, Virginia, with the Union Army on their heels.

You Are Cordially Invited to The Surrender Ceremony of Honored Guests

Robert E. Lee
and
Ulysses S. Grant

April 9, 1865
Appomattox Court House, VA

Regrets Only

hitter

Home Profile Find People Settings Help

What's happening?

Discover what battles are happening right now, anywhere in the war

Tweet!

Home

Tweet!

rebelyeller the war is over. Today is a shameful day for the South, but at least we can rest.

Northguy Union won the war! It's over!

NoGunSon finally we can celebrate peace in the United States!

Union general Ulysses S. Grant at Appomattox Court House, Virginia...President Lincoln assassination by Southerner John Wilkes Booth...Vice President

woman in the world...2006...The Covenant becomes the first black book to reach number 1 on the New York Time's nonfiction paper back best seller list... 2007...Oprah Winfrey opens the Oprah Winfrey Leadership Academy for Girls in South

Confederate Surrender at Appomattox Court House, VA

Warbook Search

NEWS FEED

Robert E. Lee is accepting his defeat gracefully
about 150 years ago.

54,215 people like this

View all 567 comments

U.S. Grant you're a good man, Lee

Jefferson Davis you fought a good fight, I'm proud of you!

Mary Custis Lee come on home now, honey.

Write a comment ...

Abraham Lincoln is so happy to put the Union back together again!
about 150 years ago.

100,000 people like this

View all 5,000 comments

John Right finally!

Mary Smith I believe in you, Lincoln!

Jim Bob even the south is glad to hear the war is over.

Write a comment ...

Even though Lee surrendered on April 9th, fighting continued for weeks until all troops got the word!

April 12, 1865

Dear Mary,

I'm coming home!! Have my bed soft and ready and a nice boiling pot of that cowboy chili you make so well. I can't wait to see you!

Your husband,
Mitchell

The Civil War produced many inventions including the rifle, machine gun, grenades, ironclad ships, submarines, and the American Red Cross.

...and that was that. The war was over. The Union won.

But in reality, both sides lost. Thousands of men were killed. By the end, most of the soldiers were weary, weak, and ready for home. The war was devastating to the country, leaving the land barren. Much of the South had to start from scratch rebuilding houses, factories, even whole cities!

Still, some good things came out of the Civil War. For one, the United States has never gone to war against itself since. You could say the Civil War made the United States a stronger country. But probably the greatest benefit of the Civil War was that slaves were freed! Shortly after the war, the 13th Amendment was added to the U.S. Constitution. The Amendment abolished slavery and made any act of slavery against the law.

The Civil War was only a small step for African Americans; they had a long road toward freedom ahead of them. African Americans fought for equal rights up into the 1960s. Still, prejudices and discriminations against African Americans happen everyday. But we've made some progress since the Civil War. We even have our first African American president!

Andrew Johnson sworn into office...John Wilkes Booth shot and killed in Bowling Green, Virginia...President Johnson submits plan for Restoration of South Africa... 2008... Barack Obama wins presidential election becoming first African American president-elect... 2009...Barack Obama is inaugurated as the first African American President ...Michelle Obama is the first African American First Lady...

Reconstruction

Reconstruction: the recovery and rebuilding period following the Civil War

Can you believe the war is finally over? The weight of the world has been lifted from my husband's shoulders. I can see it in his eyes. And we are going to Ford's Theatre to see a play tonight! A night of lighthearted fun—I cannot wait!—**Mary Todd Lincoln**

POP! What was that? Part of the play? Women are shrieking! A man has leaped onto the stage, yelled, and run off. The president slumps in his chair! I see blood! Can it be true?! Did someone just shoot our president?!—**usher**, Ford's Theatre

Stop that man!—**Major Henry Rathbone**

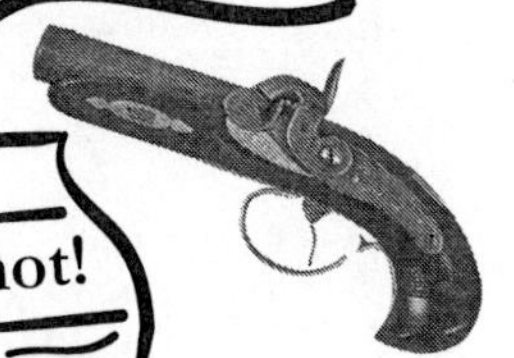

Everyone is sobbing. Our president died early this morning. May God have mercy on this country.—**newspaper reporter**

I accept this office of President of the United States with a heavy heart.—Vice President **Andrew Johnson**

He was in that barn and wouldn't come out. So we set it on fire! I saw my chance, and took it. I shot him. I shot and killed that John Wilkes Booth.—**Union soldier***

*The manhunt for John Wilkes Booth was the largest in history, involving 10,000 federal troops, detectives, and police.

Here are the latest statistics, Sir: 618,000 soldiers dead; probably 100,000 civilians killed too, Sir. That includes the North and South, Sir. And we know that disease killed twice as many as those who died in battle.—**Union soldier** *

*The Civil War death toll is more than the total killed in battle in the American Revolution, War of 1812, Mexican War, Spanish-American War, World War I, World War II, Korean War, Vietnam, and Gulf War—all combined!

The Legend of *Taps*

In 1862, Union Army Captain Robert Ellicombe looked over the battle scene. He heard the groan of a wounded soldier. Although, he did not know if the soldier was a Union soldier or a Confederate soldier, the captain crawled through the battle amidst gunfire and carried the soldier to the medical tent. When he got back, he found that the soldier was a Confederate, but he was already dead. He recognized the face of the soldier and realized it was his own son. Because the son was a Rebel, he was not allowed to have a full military burial. Only one musician, a bugler, was allowed to play. The father asked the bugler to play a song that was found in the pocket of his son's uniform. The bugler played the song that became known as *Taps*.

This story is legend, not historically accurate

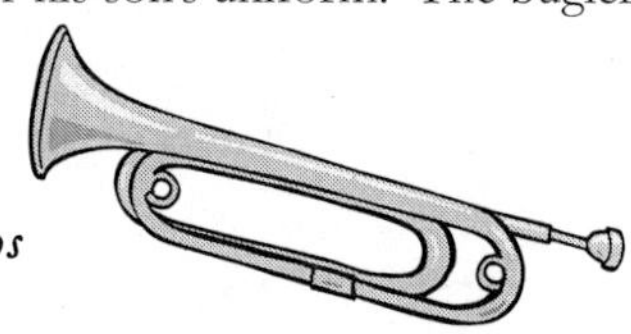

The True Story of *Taps*

General Daniel Butterfield was dissatisfied with the customary firing of three rifles at the end of military burials. He altered a French bugle call into what is now known as *Taps*. The song became very popular, and within months it was sounded by both the Union and Confederate armies.

This story is the true story of *Taps*. Not as fun and romantic as the Legend!

When we said our vows years ago, I was just a child. Jefferson was 18 years my elder. My momma almost cried when I said I wanted to marry him. But we've had a happy life together. Full of struggles, I suppose, but happy. I never thought I'd be the First Lady of the Confederacy, not in a million years! But I stand by Jefferson in everything. Right now he's locked up, accused of treason since the great South lost this Civil War. But I'm staying right here outside his jail cell. I'll fight for his release until I feel him back in my arms again, no matter how long it takes.—**Varina Howell Davis***

*Jefferson Davis was released in 1867 thanks to his wife's unrelenting requests for his freedom.

Everything is destroyed! Houses burned. Fields barren. Animals dead or dying—I can count their ribs. What has happened to our beautiful South?—**Confederate soldier**

My lifeless body hangs on the scaffold. Three guilty men wave in the wind beside me. They accused me of conspiring to kill Abraham Lincoln. I did no such thing!—ghost of **Mary Surratt**

If these old walls could talk, they would tell a history so fascinating and terrifying, no student would ever tire of learning about American events. I was built years ago, before any of these men were even born. My walls were erected for protection, but just look at them now. Spirits seem to haunt this sad and forlorn place, and will forever more.—**Fort Monroe**

...All Confederate states except Mississippi readmitted to Union...Six Confederate officers form anti-black society, Ku Klux Klan...1866...Congress passes Civil

Susan Rice is the first African American woman to become the United States' U.N. Ambassador...Eric Holder is the first African American Attorney General of the United States...50-year-old pop icon Michael Jackson dies of cardiac arres t...Venus

Did I ever think I would see this day? No, sir! No more slavery—thanks to the Thirteenth Amendment to the Constitution. What a day, what a day! Free at last! Praise the Lord!—**former slave**

We've got to keep these free blacks under control! We'll wear white robes and hoods and terrorize them at night—they'll think we're spirits of Confederate soldiers! That'll keep them in their place.—**Ku Klux Klan member***

*The Ku Klux Klan was a secret society organized by Southerners that used violence and terror to maintain "white supremacy."

I thought the war was over! But they passed that Military Reconstruction Act and Union troops are still here—occupying the South! It's like pouring salt into a fresh wound. And those Northerners wonder why we're bitter?!—**Southern schoolteacher**

Carpetbaggers! Scalawags! Just look at them taking advantage of our pain to make money for themselves! Why, if one of them comes into my shop, I'll shoo him out so fast his hat will spin right off his head!—**Southern shopkeeper**

Thank ya, suh for these clothes to wear and food for my fam'ly. We have nothin'. Don't know what we'd do without the Freedman's Bureau to help us. It seems like everyone else is ag'in us.—**freed slave***

*The Freedman's Bureau was a federal agency formed to help former slaves get food, clothing, medical care, and fair treatment after the war.

Tenants ain't got no chance. I don't know who gets the money, but it ain't the poor. It gets worse every year—the land gets more wore out, the price for tobacco gets lower, and everything you got to buy gets higher. Like I said, I'm trying to 'be content' like the Bible says and not to worry, but I don't see no hope.—**sharecropper's wife**

We have great hopes for the Fourteenth Amendment! It grants equality to all citizens, but big problems still exist between blacks and whites in the South. Southern states have passed Black Codes—laws to deny former slaves their rights. There is still such violence…will they ever embrace each other?—**Northern Congressman**

So far from engaging in a war to perpetuate slavery, I am rejoiced that slavery is abolished. I believe it will be greatly for the interest of the South. So fully am I satisfied of this that I would have cheerfully lost all that I have lost by the war and have suffered all that I have suffered to have this object obtained.—**Robert E. Lee***

*Robert E. Lee spent the rest of his life as President of Washington and Lee University in Lexington, Virginia

I cannot help but feel sad and depressed…at the downfall of a foe who fought so long and valiantly, and had suffered so much for a cause, though that cause was, I believe, one of the worst for which people ever fought.—**Ulysses S. Grant**

Today, I have been elected to the United States Senate! I'm the first black man elected to the U.S. Senate! I must work to protect the rights of my black brethren. They have a steep hill to climb.— **Hiram Revels**, Mississippi

I'll be the first black man to cast my vote after the Fifteenth Amendment grants blacks the right to vote. My parents were slaves…and here I am! What a privilege! What an honor! I can't wait to vote!—**Thomas Mundy Peterson**

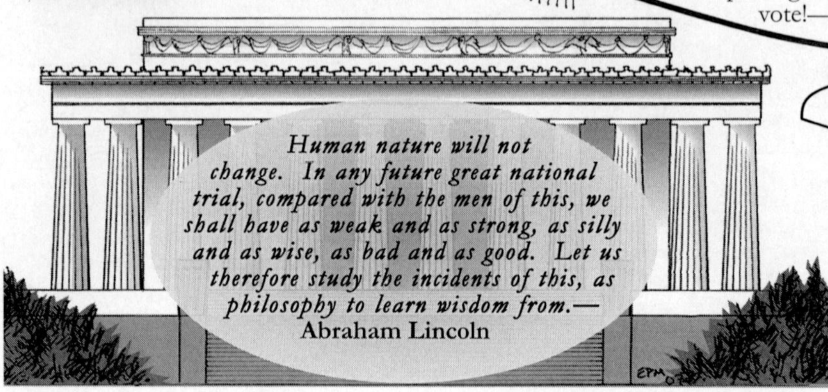

***Human nature will not change. In any future great national trial, compared with the men of this, we shall have as weak and as strong, as silly and as wise, as bad and as good. Let us therefore study the incidents of this, as philosophy to learn wisdom from.*—**
Abraham Lincoln

g'night John Boy
g'night Mama
g'night Tecumseh
g'night Robert E.
g'…
g'night Stonewall
Lights out, boys!

Rights Act…1868…14th Amendment to the Constitution guarantees equal rights…1870…15th Amendment grants blacks right to vote.

and Serena Williams are the first African American world doubles tennis champions…Disney unveils The Princess and the Frog, the studio's first animated film featuring an African American princess.